Woman Crossing a Field

Woman Crossing a Field

POEMS BY
Deena Linett

American Poets Continuum Series, No. 99

BOA Editions, Ltd. ❖ Rochester, NY ❖ 2006

First Edition
06 07 08 09   7 6 5 4 3 2 1

Publications by BOA Editions, Ltd.—
a not-for-profit corporation under section 501 (c) (3)
of the United States Internal Revenue Code—
are made possible with the assistance of grants from
the Literature Program of the New York State Council on the Arts;
the Literature Program of the National Endowment for the Arts;
the Sonia Raiziss Giop Charitable Foundation; the Lannan Foundation;
the Mary S. Mulligan Charitable Trust; the County of Monroe, NY;
the Rochester Area Community Foundation;
the Elizabeth F. Cheney Foundation; the Ames-Amzalak Memorial Trust
in memory of Henry Ames, Semon Amzalak and Dan Amzalak;
the Chadwick-Loher Foundation in honor of Charles Simic and Ray Gonzalez;
the Steeple-Jack Fund; the Chesonis Family Foundation,
as well as contributions from many individuals nationwide.

See Colophon on page 116 for special individual acknowledgments.

Cover Design: Lisa Mauro
Cover Art: "VanBuskirk Angel" by Anique Taylor, courtesy of the artist
Interior Design and Composition: Richard Foerster
Manufacturing: McNaughton & Gunn
BOA Logo: Mirko

Library of Congress Cataloging-in-Publication Data

Linett, Deena, 1938–
    Woman crossing a field : poems / by Deena Linett.— 1st ed.
        p. cm. — (American poets continuum series ; v. 99)
    ISBN 1–929918–79–8 (pbk. : alk. paper)
    I. Title. II. Series.

PS3562.I514W66 2006
811'.54—dc22

2005030034

NATIONAL
ENDOWMENT
FOR THE ARTS

BOA Editions, Ltd.
Thom Ward, Editor
David Oliveiri, Chair
A. Poulin, Jr., President & Founder (1938–1996)
260 East Avenue, Rochester, NY 14604
www.boaeditions.org

State of the Arts

NYSCA

for Ruth Aoife,

       one grain of pollen from the endless vast tree of the world

Contents

Altarpiece

Time, Grasses

I don't need your praise
to survive. I was here first,
before you were here, before
you ever planted a garden.
And I'll be here when only the sun and moon
are left, and the sea, and the wide field.

I will constitute the field.

"Witchgrass"
—Louise Glück, *The Wild Iris*

Time, Grasses

From here it seems she stands alone on a steep slope,
wind blowing the grasses over. She is naked, lean,

gazes at the sun, unflinching. In sleet and snow
and rain she stands, and when ice falls in little stones

and blows. Day and night, naked before all of it.
She is young, and does not look ahead, or down.

Or up. Years go. She is not stone, so
does not erode. Nor is she light, to be diminished.

A crude rendering of soul, she is raw
material endowed with fear and feeling, unflinching

error. You know her, a tree, a stream, a living
sentience that hurtling downhill sends up sparkles.

These do not emanate from her but are reflected
matter as it meets her temporary body, solid, liquid, air.

Fields of Light

Bright Yellow Square: Laib's Pollen

Hirschhorn Museum

We looked up for the source of the light. We do this
all the time, behave as if a thing we know is not
quite clearly there before us, love or fury. A square
of brightness on the floor like a window onto something.
We imagined he had pulled it down and gathered it,
staggered home with it—all that light in his arms!
through the terrible fields of Germany—organic smudge
which once had been a cube of summer bearing memories
of meadows, spans of wild grasses flattened to a plane
of light. We studied it as if it were a mystery laid bare,
as if by steady looking we could see the way it bore
some necessary information, how to live perhaps, how to bear
the weight of everything that happens, grain by grain.

Revision

to the man in "True North"

It was south, actually, and you were more self-conscious
probably than I could know. I could barely speak.

We spoke. In a story I wrote before I knew you
the married woman buys handmade underwear for her tryst,

blue silk, like a night with too few stars to tell direction,
not a breath of hesitation as piece by piece she takes it off,

balls it up and drops it in the wastebasket
in the hotel room after he leaves. No hotel room.

We ate in full view of dozens of people
not paying attention. You leaned toward me,

eyes burning, your face obliterating all my work,
my children, entire histories. I ate eggs,

soft food that doesn't need much chewing.
No one watching could have known. How could I know

it would cost me everything? You can't know
the last time you see him it will be the last time.

Woman in the Garden

At the Isabella Stewart Gardner Museum in Jamaica Plain, Massachusetts, a headless statue faces away from tables where, in spring, visitors can sit under the trees chatting over their tea and little cakes.

She can't think of him: she's lost her head,
has given us, so to speak, the cold shoulder.

In this way I will turn from you
implacable as marble, less porous.

Fictions of Place–Time

If a woman stands in the middle of Massachusetts Avenue
facing MIT [but in memory is so firmly] in the village of
LeRaincy that she is . . . oblivious to the cars around her
and so is hit, run over, killed . . . is she more truly in
Boston or in France when she dies?

—Janette Turner Hospital, *Charades*

Suppose you were born to Overseas French
visiting in Christchurch on the twenty-first of March

came north and west to manhood in the States:
on what day would your birthday fall and in what language,

in what season? My son sleeps in L.A. with his new wife
in full light where the coast curves east to meet the dawn

and here in San Francisco where I am today it's barely light
enough to see the gray-green eucalyptus or any of the palms.

In Beijing and Khe Sanh, days that haven't happened yet
along the California coast are more than halfway gone

and any night an ancient Maori music might play erotic tunes
against your bones, drumming out the need for water.

Before the onrush of the formal dark, traces of the rage
to say *place and time are mere ideas. This* is where

—and when—we were together or apart, lived out
the little dramas of our lives, the surrounds beautiful or vacant.

Above Half-Moon Bay

California, July '01, with Chris

We walked sun-bleached grasses along rifts
and splits devised by earthquake on a cliff-

edge above the blue, space between east
and west, the idea and the perfect sentence, now

and now. I dropped a penny in a slit
where a crevice opened at the verge

of the sea: cracks ramified like root-hairs,
like rivulets, as water goes to every compass point

when the earth rolls; design like silver tracks
thought makes as it runs; tributaries, blood flow,

course of capillaries, fault-lines, scissures.
Like nothing but themselves. No thud,

and the Pacific marine-blue all the way to Tokyo.
Wildflowers, yellow, blue, and red; thistles

I thought only grew in Scotland, but pricked
my finger and it bled. No wakening or prince.

This is how my life goes, tilting, riven,
episodic in ways unacceptable in a novel,

long stretches when nothing happens.
Found a branch of small pods filled with air

—animal or veg? Seaweed like thread
from tapestry goes brittle, as shells and stones

lifted from the water lose their color, as we
are stripped of language far from home.

That long fall to the scalding fluid heart, scruple
of copper melting into gold and boiling mud

from the time before we had been dreamed of,
the entire universe the size of a stadium:

Roman, Christians, and lions. Now
Afghan women shot and all of us shapes

of willful longing adrift over the face
of the earth, starry dust, seed, and spore.

Fårösund

Blue seas icy-bright and splashed with light
in summer. On Fårö stunted pine, sharp wind,

beaches' long deep reaches to the water.
Rock shelves struck by limestone stele

taller than a man and pocked with glitter,
veins of cream and red and green

laid down by impulses long stilled. Glare
makes seeing it up close impossible,

and none of it shows: grief, night-sweats, urges
and the sudden yielding, acts whose origins

remain obscure to those who lived them.
Clouds drift east toward Latvia, toward Turku.

Out of the Garden

Stone and leaded glass, brick. Green vistas. Praise,
doubt's opposite or double, pulls buildings hard to earth.
We walk through ornamental seminary gates

along a promenade of trees, gates
to purple hills. Evening sun like praise
falls on our portion—incomprehensible earth—

strokes skin to heated sweetness and the earth
cools. Remember me. Look: beyond the gates
the visible world sings psalms of praise.

Earth's gardens beyond praise, our time gated.

The Mirror

She reads in Scandinavian mythology: *Did something happen?*
She's written several times of child sacrifice. Time to look
to her own stories, time to look in the mirror. The glass is livid,

silver, black, and will not yield. It has taken more than half a
      century
—longer than most people in all history have lived—to have come
this far, which is not very, to a doorway. She gazes at a room

grand and wide and full of light. Pale furniture against pale walls.
Tall windows. A room more marvelous than any she has occupied,
designed for comfort, to impress—like rooms at Drottningholm,

but brighter, and the sun more constant. The rooms are broad
and clean; she infers, then, they must be her fault, the damages,
some insufficiency, profound and ineradicable. So she comes to
      believe

in original sin, believes in this as she believes in God, though
      her god
does not require it. Sometimes she can nearly recollect the first
      words
she could read, could write, the texture of those terrifying early days

in school, fat muddy-colored beads, the long green sticky strand
to string them on. She almost believes if it were possible to scrape
the silver and the black paint from the mirror she'd be able to see

all the way back, down the long allée lined with palms in pools
of shattered shell, into fields of scrub palmetto and bamboo, all
      the way
to the Gulf. It is infinitely long and she knows now, no rooms at
      the end of it.

Devotions

Demeter at the Yellowstone

Fields. As far as she can see, grasses bend in wind.
The mother wants to gather them in mortal arms. She wishes
she were able to forget the day in the Montana mountains
when with a glimmer like a holy thing the daughter
disappeared along a rocky ledge above a waterfall
cutting stacks of angled sandstone tall as trees.
Crablike, the girl had followed it around a bend
beyond where Demeter could see. She'd watched
water sending rainbows over rock, hands empty,
and the sky, then turned from all that sparkling foam
and spray. Had the child slid down sheets of sunlit water
onto stone, the mother would have had to watch her go.

Three Small Songs

From my sixth-floor window it seems the geese
fling themselves open like arms in gesture,
become a ragged oval, then pull into something
resembling form, like us after the terrible time.
Time of the heart is a long arc. Birds' flight
promises a settling. That's not what happens.
They fan upwards and apart, break into pieces.

> *I mean the years are like a lead fence.*
> —HD

No and *no*. *No*. From one loved absolutely.
Following, many things happen, none
of them thick or thin enough for words.
No blood falls. The tides keep their appointments
and in her mouth a taste like pennies tossed
at an open violin-case underneath a bridge
(water, stink of urine-stained concrete),
or dropped into a battered coffee-can.
She is a teacup through whose thin skin
light and shadow. So knowledge comes,
fine razory grass, supple in the wind, useful
and productive, even beautiful.

It doesn't matter that you didn't know. You know
now: what happened was determined partly by your nature:
to ask the names of elements that shaped it—base
and noble elements—absurd. They're volatile, inert,
combustible, not found in nature, light, heavy; natural.
They hold the planet like the memory of an embrace.
All the great religions promise mercy, pardon, exculpation.

Whitby Abbey

658(?) • Caedmon, at the new abbey in Strenœshalc
(Whitby), makes verses, and is thought to be the first poet
in English

He was easier with language, which was simpler then.
There weren't words like *Anabaptist* in it
or *reciprocating engine.* There weren't a lot of concepts—
the basic ones did well enough: *I want, food; danger*
which became in later days *hatred. God, sex,*
big animal, and *fire* were basically all one.
With levers, pulleys, ropes, belief, soon men
would do enormous things with stone. Domes
would be invented, but he would not have heard of them.
Men had not yet found polyphony or assembled
the shapes of the world, but plainsong sounded
on the cool rough stones and flew
through narrow windows shaped like arrows
toward the foam on the sea, which it resembled.

Cathedral

For hours I held one of my son's infant twins
while she slept. For a little time
before we knew who each would be
it didn't matter which soft sweaty newborn head
lay on my breast ruining my velvet shirt.
There was nothing else in all the world I wanted.
As on approach to Chartres: it's been there centuries,
you merely have not known it. Now you know
nothing can prepare you for the way it rises
from the hills, imperfect, beautiful.
Nothing is required of you, and everything.

Holy Saturday in the Northern Plains

for my daughter

A mild day. The Mississippi runs flat and blue and gray
between reddish grasses and pale fallow fields.
In sun your great-grandmothers' diamonds splinter light
into component possibilities: spikes of blue and red
and yellow; green. In a time when few Jews
know their grandmothers, we have these that send up plumes
of light, all there is of immortality, bits of carbon
freed of local dust and rinsed of history. Or this:
one dyed blond hair I lift from my sleeve and set out
on the little wind. I'd like to think a bird whose call
sounds more like a machine than song will add it to her home
of mud and grasses a thousand miles from where I live,
in limbs of cottonwood or aspen. Look: three geese
streak like something marvelous above our emblematic river.

Generation

How things come together: a solstice and the moon at perigee.
All over America my children go out into radiant cold light to see
and call to tell me on the telephone. As they speak it comes to me

how remarkable this is: I have dedicated a book of poems to
identical twin granddaughters just now years away from reading,
    who
will need decades to understand the syntax in it, and the love
    and sex.

Scribbling on scraps of colored paper and the backs of checks,
I've longed to know if my grandmothers grieved their age
as I do. I am older now than my grandmother was when I slept

in her room alert to the rough irregular course of her breath
in the other bed, certain she would die—what would I do with
    death?
The moonlight carved sharp folds into linens stiff

as her closed-off Yiddish-speaking self. The other grandmother,
slightly less reserved, perhaps bequeathed me her formality,
a silver serving spoon, a diamond watch I've given to my daughter.

They could never have imagined this, a book, as I cannot
    imagine them moist
and young, legs parted, bearing; as I could not imagine me, a
    hinge joining
five generations, my mother's image glinting off the angles of
    my face, my flesh

the stuff of hers whose scent and mystery retain a living freshness
though I grow older now than she had lived to be. Time's
      vertical slash
finds me at the center; at horizontal, on the picture plane's
      bright edge.

Two Poppies

End of winter. I buy poppies, stand them in a purple vase
that glows in sun and carry it from room to room
all through my day. Above a squiggle
like a question mark in the tall hairy stem, a yellow bowl
the size of my hand, edges notched, ruckled, rippled,
translucent—like early Roman mouth-blown glass—
loud chartreuse at center, and little swipes of orange,
as if a realist had gone mad with paint. Wrinkled red silk,
the other seems half-born, a fabled animal unfolding
from the split seedpod, its caul, like the calf
I saw emerging from its mother at the side of a road
onto stones and flower-studded grasses near Kirkwall.
Like my daughter and me at the beach: I remember we bent,
each to her book, one facing east to the sea, one west.

The Archimedes Palimpsest

for Aimée

Once upon a time in Syracuse a boy grew
into manhood keen to study, so found
the value of π. It is believed
that like Einstein he thought in images.
[You're not supposed to mix rhetorics, but]
Picture this: he wanted to understand
the maths of movement, which is change.
Imagine Freud. Imagine the monk

who laid two columns of a Christian text
on vellum with old writing on it, turned
the leaves, inscribed his new words
at right angles to a faded script and added
prayers the brothers made, and chants.

Two thousand years went by. [We don't know
where they go; the language doesn't offer. Time
passes—into what? It may be looped like bolts
of cloth or rooted in vast meadows, folded;
or lie in heaps somewhere, to be collected.]
A thousand years till glass is used for windows.

Brothers dripped wax onto his sacred text
and added sketches—the Evangelists—
and pigment. And Time itself is injury,
edges wore, were cut, words rubbed away,
were overlaid by paint and drops of spittle,
mildew, burns, and spatterings of blood.
The brothers' singing through cold nights
over centuries didn't mark folios notched

by early compasses (but in imagination
we can hear them), runnels, blots, and scrapes,
leaves scored by their petitions, visions, dreams.

Chance dances through and over twenty centuries:
the single instance of this book in all the world
is found—twice!—its medieval Latin Christian text
laid across the ancient Greek: warp and weft,

faith and science. Toward the end of my century
X-rays and spectrometers have been invented:
now we can see, decode, decipher. In visible
light—and under infrared and ultraviolet—defects
yield diagrams that reach toward knowledge of infinity.

Of the various infinities—we know now—some
are larger than others. Despite the way we think
that everything has changed, Archimedes died
when soldiers broke down his doors,
killed him, and the book of his life was lost.

Photograph: Am Naschmarkt

Unattributed. Vienna ca. 1910

The woman is a milliner. She will never hear of Freud
or dance at fests her city will be famous for

in times to come. She sews on brilliants, bits
of satin ribbon, buttons faceted to catch the light, sits

in the sun, fifty and massive as furniture. Sheets
of butcher-paper line the splintered tabletop

on which flowers have been scattered. Strips of lace
and sunlight stripe hatboxes filled with cards of pins

and silken folds. A linen rose has slipped onto her lap.
Her gaze in the broad face is quick, unlettered, rapt.

Perhaps she watches for her man, or waits
for her daughter to come back with a plum

—a taste for fruit plagues the mother of late.
Photographs deny soft flesh and wetness. A stock

of little wicker baskets she is keeping for a friend
is streaked by sun. You can see that they were stacked

but now have fallen, light and dark. She has no future:
she's a woman in a photograph, looks past us.

Arnold's Meadow

The mown span's a rock-strewn incline, matchless,
imperfect: tall dry stalks, wind-blasted trees
and plumy grasses, rotting fruit. Cultivated iris beds
line the western edge and in their cycles roses,
allium and lilies, everything exclaiming.
A century-old apple tree, small copy of the great world-tree,
sets out globes of red and gold composed of memories
of wind and snow and sunlight. In ponds of greeny water
dark as amnion, koi marked like Saint Bernards
before they're mammals flash black and white and gold
between the water grasses. Little tracts of scum
blotch images of cloud astride the unstill surface
like wishes or intention and never come ashore.
All day the light on bark and leaf and water.

Homage to Rothko

Guide to the Cathedral

Here we have a small cathedral, made like prayer
from natural materials. See, the floors and sills
have been composed of blood and excrement, with wine
in varying amounts according to the workmen's whim.
Observe the gleaming doors and wreath-ringed pillars;
glass in the confessional is bluer than a newborn's eye
and clear as snowmelt. The gilded spire's a miracle
of engineering, and archways trimmed in gold
contain the fire that does not consume. Floral
arrangements are replaced daily. These
are particularly lovely, textured lilies purest white,
red tulips with their little stripes of blue
and flounces at the edge. The carved stone roses
were made by prisoners in need of something beautiful.

Aerial Map: Everglades

53 Km NW of Miami (computer image)

You watch the grid fill in as if
it would yield information you can use:
looks like 60-year-old linoleum
with milk spilled on it. I follow
an irregular diagonal like a hair
under a microscope till finally
it resolves to water. "River of Grass"
more truly is a shallow sea,
streams of salty water, sweet,
pools sustaining herons, egrets,
moccasins. Morning's cool mists
drift above the sawgrass
and the shattered shell, slip
between the trunks of mangrove,
water nymphs emerging
from imagination, seductive
and beseeching. The panthers
are mostly gone now. From here
where the satellite's eye stares,
all that struggle underneath's
not visible, all that dying, all that
hunger and revival, call and song,
sounds that rise at night
from the camp-meeting ground
onto the permanent summer.

Rothko

And if he'd never left Latvia? If his father the wolf
had caught him by his furry neck and rolled him in snow,
if he had never held a paintbrush? Or if an eagle stole him
from his cradle in a sunlit spot and left him in a world
of gray and black and white, the odd red berry like a drop
of fox-blood on the snow? The leering green of spring
and sounds of rushing water brief here where wind
tears into Russia from the north. The boy knew all of it,

pastureland, the grids of towns, bridges where the Daugava
runs south out of the Baltic, hills thick with birches, fields
like gold-leaf shivering, ice-fast evergreens, the stillness
and the dread. Color rises out of landscape, frames
cities planned on civil grounds with civil reason, renders
states, their borders porous as reality. Moscow to the east,
Helsinki north. Vilna and Vitebsk. Forests,
harbors, islands. He looked up to emptiness and blue.

Retrospective: Works on Paper

December 1996

I make three copies of the photograph
—probably taken by a woman—
that accompanies the exhibition,
work made by a man I loved, now dead.
Subtlety does not survive
reproduction on reproduction
by machine. From here
you can't see lively eyes
but the *bitter edge* a critic saw
—and that I touched—is there.
Articles tell a life: born here, died
there, achievement and the arc
of recognition unpredictable; the dark.
As if a list could show a man
in all his complex possibilities, taut
and flexible. Younger then
than when I shared his bed
he gazes past the edge
at something we can't see. Hard
at his back, doorways and walls echo
depth of field odd as a de Chirico.
White cotton shirt, pants crushed
into permanent creases at the groin,
the legs and ankles stained with paint,
his arm in shadow. A clutch of brushes juts
from one hand. Brightness planes
down his knuckles, strikes
the face of the watch and flies away
from the wrist I knew blue with veins.

I Sleep with a Man I Don't Love

Hold a water goblet up and fill it
to the brim with sun: reflections
sparkle on the floor, rims and sides
and bottoms dance. Amazing: the eye
distinguishes with ease the densities
in insubstantial counterparts. Therefore
it is absurd to want the softly shining light
of May at half-past six to last. Tonight
the light has pressed against my window
but not through, or it is so oblique
that by the time it meets the wall
it doesn't replicate the smirch I see on glass,
optics' tricks appealing as our own
or love's, both particles and waves
always unique and always the same.

Optics

I carry my dress from the cleaner's, flat between sheets
of plastic. It sways as I walk, its shadow in the street
phantom folds and overlays, fields of dimensionless grays;
follows me home like a friendly apparition lacking animal
or shell. Imagine having lain beneath the greeny light
of shallow seas and looked up into sun, the runneled ceiling
swelling and subsiding halls of light, brief dwelling
finer than the world of air. Imagine resting there,
on littoral's soft corrugations, stilled,
all substance pardoned. Water folds and furls, lifts,
goes, winds in insubstantial sheets your fine sheer skin.

Child on an Airplane

As she moves past my seat
my eyes stop her
forever at ten
and strangely graceful
for her age. Wide face,
thin-lidded eyes,
and bee-sting lips
she's not aware of yet.

East toward the dawn,
nearly midnight New York time,
white seeps into the sky:
in the Atlantic life's rush
lashes depths like ribbons
flung and snapped, shocks
of color in the dark.

I'm hoping for the green flash
I saw once as the sun rose
over Ecuador
painting Andes snowfields pink.
Great gifts do not repeat.
They slash the sky,
briefly blaze and clamor.

This child could be a Netherlandish
fifteenth-century madonna,
but no one has touched her yet,
no one has claimed her.

The older woman, girl
she once was furled

and motionless within,
knows what wild burgeoning
will overtake her, the way a wave
will take a swimmer out
into her dark local sea
beyond her depth, beyond breath
to precincts jeweled like fabled cities:
tossed and humbled, joyful
and amazed she'll breast
the new element, easy
in the tumble and the rush,
its fierce sweet hush.

The Dead Child

Photo, The New YorkTimes, *May 22, 1996*

can't imagine why she has been chosen,
has never heard of Isaac, and sacrifice
is not in her vocabulary or on her mind.

Taken to high places, told to pray,
she kneels. Her mother looked away
this morning, so she did not dare

embrace her. *Bare your neck.* Does
as she is told. I was in the Andes
above the treeline, at walls of stone

like those on which her small cries echoed,
child coming to awareness, buried
with the statuettes. Her stilled call

calls down centuries, right hand tight
around the coca leaves that brought no ease,
the fine wool dress, her winding sheet, still bright.

Trees in Ice

Enthralled by trees in thrall to ice,
their branches bearing all that snow
still as held breath, I am not thinking
of the gravity of loss, the weightless
heft and loft of hope,
but how their tangled crossings grow
like crystals, each its own form:
the idea of the first violin, architectures
of interiors of breasts, turns and channels
in the mind, the possibilities of symphonies.

Inlet, Duluth

Currents, chance moisture
—shadows fall haphazard
over purple grasses
streams of gray in layers
water roughened by wind—

Sky and sky. Tree.
Tree. Tree. Tree.

3 Men: Portraits Without the Human Figure

Hotel-casino: lights flash, crowds tread
patterned carpets hoping for a turn
in fortune. Despite the ardent wishes
of the women you have left you are not dead.
You're good at lively passing things
that happen here: at restaurants, in bed,
at tables tossing dice and cards. That smudge
at bottom right stands in for me, and you plunge
breathless into chance as into women, risk
like drink obliterating everything.

Studio: smells of linseed oil and turpentine. Brushes,
palette knives, mixing-sticks; bottles, jars, tubes. Paint
in daubs and gobs and smears and dots and slashes.
You left the window open and everything stained.

Greenhouse: Beneath little panes pocked
by time and dotted with mold and lichen, rot,
a riot of tropical effulgence, small framed portion
of the endlessness. Spiky plants blossom
like ideas; light glances off the glass and gleams
on the permanent hunger, steams. Everything
blooms or is green. You shrug into your coat.

Ocean Park

Series by Richard Diebenkorn

Planes and fields of greens like fields
seen from aloft, cultivated and wild,
forests, farms, blues of sea's edge,
the littoral, horizon lines, rows
of turquoise pools, the pitch and list
of houses white in sunlight, surfaces
like Earth's, leveled, angled
one against the other, laid along highways
like rope tossed and fallen, slashed
by tinsel warp of rivers, split
by long straight roads we plan
before the sudden turn, sharp cutting off.

Disquisition on Yellow

June, 1846, Cartoon, The Almanack of the Month: *J.M.W. Turner in top hat before a canvas with bucket (labeled* YELLOW*). He holds a mop:* Turner was excessive in his use of the colour yellow.

1923 book on color theory: Yellow gains in charm as we study its qualities.

Granddaughters' Playroom

The mirror twins have bent their heads
over thick paints in five small bowls.
They make *Storms with thunder* and *A nice day.*
They are four. *Yellow is the least various
color,* says Amelia. *Not* least, *protested yellow!*
Sophie says. To herself, *I wonder
what I could do to make blood color.*

Notebook

Yellow opposes dread.

Uranium oxide gives yellow and red,
my clay book says. *Iron oxide
can be roasted to deeper shades
and finally will yield red. Uranium
will produce cool lemon-yellows.*
Lemon butter, lemon tart, lemon chrome.
Add blueberries, chill and serve.
Chromate of lead yields "A new
and beautiful yellow pigment":
Blackwoods, 1819. I wonder the color

of leaks from containers of spent
fuel rods—imagine green.
Borges sees amorphous fields
of yellow, dedicates *The Gold
of the Tigers to this last most loyal
color* as his vision goes.

van Gogh Museum

Yellow harness or trapeze or net. Apparatus of alchemy
to catch him when he fell—for surely he would fall.
Yellow chair, table, bed, the light dazzles red,
thick and real as wheatfields, cypresses, and sky.

Notebook

Chromatic scale: like a little sun the raw egg
rides the bottom of your bowl astride its clear white
just before the tines spin it into foam and recollection
and delight. A child painted at the bottom waits
for you to finish but no matter how you move the spoon
the egg will always cover it—as when you try to stop
the moment sleep comes when you're eight.

Why are we mad for bursts of light?

You can hear the Sun's sounds on the web
[http://solar-center-stanford.edu/singing/singing/html]

Filaments leap from seas of flame: hoops and plumes
soar ten thousand miles from the surface, inscribe
their violent temporary scrawl beyond the skies.

[AU= Astronomical Units: Sun's distance from Earth]

I saw *The Sun in Ultraviolet Light*
broadcast from Hubble
and made small enough to apprehend:
yellow-green, swathed in gauze,
incandescent gossamer beyond imagining –

London, The Turners

As if when he opened the paints—or ground them—light
splashed out. Lead and chalk and ink and graphite; egg white,
at least a dozen yellows and several reds, and all of it

like something sifted, haze and fog and mist. Critics:
Hah! pictures of nothing. Steam and cloud, life's drift
and heave, the brilliant impermanence of shadow, its

soft indelible suggestions. As if the paints were particle
and wave—as if they were without a substance—and in a great
        dark pub
he'd ordered pints of light and poured them. I would have liked

to watch him laying in the whites and all those yellows, thumb's
quick swipes, blotting with a swab of paper or dry bread.
Some of what he knew: red and orange come from toasted lead

and you get green suspending copper over vinegar. His
is an essentially religious view, and reassuring: our lives are mist
and sunshot dust, moonlit vapor, veils and sprays

of blowing snow and salty air, a temporary gathering of whim
and changing atmospheres beneath the Sun's short crossing.

Outside Edinburgh

Little saffron-laden stamens in the crocus
and like a blush coloring the fields, poppies.

Folds and crests of hills crossed with gorse,
golden rape to the horizon: glory as crop.

Therefore,

The silken thread that leads you through the labyrinth
—and maybe out—gleams with light, is red, and made of gold.

Altarpiece

Belfast Suite

Night, Queen's Elms

Queen's University

At home the wind blusters a bit like a young tough,
then moves on. Here it hangs around Belfast Lough
like history, unsatisfied and undiminished. On my way

—Thanksgiving in my native country, drizzly, gray—
I stopped to study objects left by Roman legions
up near York two thousand years ago: there were dragons

in England—carved into ornament—and letters. Runic lines
cut into slips of birch-bark, alder. In a glass case
the body of a young man thought to be a Prince

of Ireland left unburied in a bog, his throat slit,
bits of mistletoe in his stomach in accord with Druid rite.
I imagine he came in a coracle seeking a wife,

girl with hair dark north-of-England red
that remembers its long history of black. No moon
that night to light the harrowing. They let his blood run

into the earth. Likely it was cold and there was wind and rain.

A Geography

As if someone had incised a fine detailed design
at the bottom of a hand-thrown bowl—fruit
and flowers, little figures cutting turf, stopping

in at neighbors' to tell joy or trouble, meeting
in the streets—and following the upward curves,
had laid out stone-strewn fields and rivers, so the city

climbs from the floor of a broad shallow valley,
crowded stretches desperate for a bit of green,
to hilly precincts dense with shrubs beneath great trees.

In winter mist, forms wavering like will gather
particularity from shadows the color of bruises.
And then, sweet gift: the sun tosses her gilded shawl

on all of it, rows of smoke-black brick gleam in the wet,
grand houses, streams of crowded noisy flats, as if
all of it were joined at last beneath contending skies.

Linear

*In the interests of security it may be necessary
to close the doors of the museum. Visitors
are admitted at the risk of such temporary detention.*

—Sign at entrance, the Ulster Museum

*The power loom was invented in 1785;
by 1870 there were 15,000 power looms in Ulster.*

Taller than a man, wide, these were the pride of Empire
and their owners: tooth and roller, spike and wire,
gear and pinion. At the end of a terrible century
and silenced for a hundred years, they terrify.
The girls who served them hover in an awful din
in the stillness.
        Before the fires are made they rise
in the dark, smooth on petticoats, fasten stays. All the days
but Sunday bend to the work, dreaming young men,
lopsided smiles, whistled tunes, startling hands, scarlet
poppies all the way to the horizon and scatterings of blooms
—yarrow, thistle, mallow—like a fever of desire, the flax
like fallen summer. And do as they are driven, tend the looms.

Anniversary Photo

Belfast Telegraph

You see the arm first, elbow angled into the foreground,
the watch heavy on a narrow wrist resting on the shoulder
of the young man. A strange embrace: the posture tells you
something's off; there is perhaps a certain stiffness.
The color picture like a banner headline runs the width
of the front page. When did I notice her eyes?
Nearly twenty-two, she is blond and beautiful, blind,
was in Omagh when the bomb went. The photo
does what pictures do, tells a little portion of the story: omits
the day itself, the blast, whoever planned and planted it.
Leaves out all the days between that day and now
and all the nights. However long she lives, every day since.

Funeral Procession

Waves of silent men pour through the streets in flood,
salt sweat and blood, behind another casket. Sun
glinting off white shirts burns eyes. Not far away
light-spattered waves wash edges of the island,
pull and release that takes its own way absolutely,
scatters sunlit foam. As if it were the world's bell
struck, stone rings to strides, clatter of grief
and righteousness. Ruddy hands on coffin, free fists
beat the air. Picking up a limb, the many-legged beast
swings into resolution, sways a bit, rights itself
and hauls its body forward, grass in the wind.

Celebration

Death like a shopper wrapped against the rain moves
into shadow for a little time. Christmas is coming,
and the millennium: buildings swagged with lights, music

pours from shops and stands. The Royal Mail's set out a truck
with loud recordings, kids play whistles and harmonicas
along the streets beneath thin temporary shelter.

All the surfaces are wet and shatter the reflected light
like jewels nobody needs and everyone's enjoying.
From a tent near City Hall, skaters' circling silhouettes

spin onto gleaming streets, shades loosed from nation
and belief and soaring on the longest night: Belfast, end
of the century. The red electric clock counts down the hours

as if we were not rushing, each toward our own deaths,
as if we won't leave dirty clothes behind, and photographs
of strangers, weeks-old blooms in scummy water.

You always knew you wouldn't get to choose the Sunday
in Paris. You remember praying for your mother, dying,
knowing finally that death had come and was acceptable.

This was a kind of gift, and not a choice. You let her go.

Isle of Lewis

58° 31' N, 6° 16.1' W.

Woman Crossing a Field

No map can render these hills, the way they fill
your field of vision, gain mass and volume
as you climb, rise to rocky paths and fall

to streams and sea. I want to know the taste
of water and the color of the house
where roadway ends. Here's the world's work,

erasing and reforming bays and inlets, coves,
filling sea-lochs, grinding stone. Charts show
a string of small spits north to south as if a beast

had taken a great breath and gone beneath,
leaving bony spines to show he's been,
and here am I, fruit and fruitful, chance seed

strewn by species, just now landed on a dot of stone
out in the ocean. What's the third side of the triform shape
steep slope and sky suggest? Not the little figure

of a woman leaning up into a hill dazed by effort
and the wind, the angle and the sun. Time,
perhaps. All of it is here if we knew how to read it,

the bog a thin pelt over stone. Above, cloud heaped up
like silver palaces, like mind volitionless: she climbs
against the pull of earth, momentum and familiar thrust

and heaves through sun-shot wind and into the next moment.
World offers itself like a lover. The fields are infinite
and patient. The word's *abandon*, noun and verb.

World

Say you drop a line into the sea: how many
meters, miles, fathoms, feet? She recalls

a strange dark June fog in New York:
across the river, buildings dark at tops

and bright below, as if the subway gratings
briefly were unbarred and allowed a little passage

of the light, her work to show it.
Washed in light as we might wish to be,

a moment's glory. We know the earth
beneath the sea is scarred and ridged

like windy hills on Lewis, and to the west
beneath the waves, the Rockall Rise, vast

trenches that must reach the heated heart.
The line rides currents to a nearby coast, snags

on stones or feathers, scattered bones,
follows the same impulse as causes notes

to ride in bottles. No wonder!
We are all charm—imaginative upshot

of the natural world, as nothing is not: this page,
these words, my breath on your cheek, in your mouth.

Opening Day, the Bridge to Dun Eistean

Detail. Underpainting
with self-portrait and artist's
signature lower right.

They come as they have always gathered here
at the verges of the sea, congregations of the faithful

and the lost. The pipes sing out above the wind
to simmering skies, and no trees listen.

As we were lifted from between our mothers' thighs
people rise from folds of hills and into visibility

at the horizon; children break from them
to tear toward where the rock falls sixty feet

to ocean. Where islands meet the foam
—like places life comes up to death—

is not a well-marked boundary. Land slumps
like hot glass to the sea, sticks a finger in, or promontory,

tosses a few islands, cuts in bays and inlets,
lets itself in softly or with storms, carves sandy scarps

like pieces of a giant puzzle knocked apart
and reassembled into forms that in our small span

seem complete. Nothing can convey, not maps,
or photographs, the British Ordnance Survey

with its famous fine detail, bridges, pubs and churches,
pink stone castles, standing stones. In Stornoway

(signs spell it in a range of ways, Steòrnabhaigh,
Steòrnabhagh), an exhibit sets out site plans,

elevations, photographs of men, their full weight
leaning into rope-slings bolted to the stone

and lowering the bridge—bright trusses
painted green—across the sea-washed notch

to connect the mainland to Dun Eistean, hillock
buckled to a lumpy peak in ice-green seas.

It's necessary here to offer minimal resistance
to the wind. The few thin metal struts support

a narrow walkway made of mesh stretched
above black water-dashed Lewisian gneiss.

Gayle isn't keen to cross it and birds go frantic
at our company. We climb. The land lifts

and swells, falls in ripples, runnels, dips, as if
it couldn't bear to part with water. In the slit

between the larger island and the rocky spit
seas spill and foam, and it's as if

a mother and her child stood in ocean holding ropes
of water, legs splayed against the currents

that must always rush between them. Look now,
that girl just come over the hill headlong: see, she trips

and falls and hauls up laughing, heedless of stones
and trouble, brushing dust from her clothes

as she runs. In the middle distance—all the days
are now—the girl's become a mother, young and lusty.

Close, the rolling gait shows bones are crumbling; wind
stirs white hair. Her lips have narrowed with the effort

of the hike and years of keeping still, but ah, her history
is tasty! Like batter pocked with fruit bits, hard

to the teeth, sharp and sweet: loved men, children
when they haven't shamed and wounded, skies like glory.

She has learned that effort, pushed to its far limits,
may not be sufficient, and the century just past

that told her if she understood things she could fix them lied.
It is not possible to see (but she can see, clear as water

filtering through bogs for centuries and safe enough
to drink), how she stood, nights, with boys

at the corner of her childhood: ice cream,
the current of excitement at being out so late,

circling bugs light-drunk, and the boys, that rush
like rivers in the sea that changes everything. Pairs

and families stream over the hills. The piper plays,
the minister will speak. In all directions icy seas,

steep stone and wild flowering things, children
teasing parents and the old breathless.

There will be sudden watercourses and deep braes,
no way to cross them. She knows now:

she has failed at everything that matters. All of it
remains unknowable and will not bend. She wants

the names for wheat-green stems with little purple caps on,
wide-bladed, and the narrow, fretting in the wind.

*Underpainting: Gayle and Joffy, Tolsta Chaolais, Isle of
Lewis, tell me Lewisian gneiss is the most ancient rock on
earth. I am grateful for their many kindnesses to me on their
home island; and to George, who says that in Lincolnshire
they call multicolored sugar sprinkles for ice cream hundreds
and thousands. I'd like hundreds and thousands, please. Love,
Deena*

Orkney Crossing

KOI

At my window between the fuselage and struts, a man
pulls a strap from the prop and sets the engine whirling—
the thrill and terror of real flying! We climb

through wind and glare into cloud like curdled pudding. Broad
stencil on the wing declares NO STEP. God
must be happy keeping such bright blues and russets

in his sight. Loch Ness nearly cuts the countryside in two:
inches of land prevent the north from floating free
of England. To fly from Glasgow to Kirkwall

—195 nautical miles—takes an hour: there it is, low
in the water, tan and brown and green and gold,
sandy slopes at sea's edge, Orkney's islands flung

like leaves of a long story. Promised to the king
in 1490, Margaret brought them as her dowry
but she sickened on her way and died. She was thirteen.

A village name recalls her having been, St Margaret's Hope.
The shadow of our little plane's a blur on water, foam
like lace at all the windows. Like body my soul travels in,

it lifts and quivers in the shimmering blue dome. Below,
waves ablaze with icy light, the jeweled green ocean
full of life and darkness and a spattering of islands. NO STEP.

A Few Facts

Forty-eight miles north to south, the biggest island, sea-girt
Mainland, climbs from easy echoes of sea-swells
to breakneck braes, and the few trees live in declivities
I thought at first were riverbeds. Norn, a form of Norse,
has given names to places. Hazel drives the few roads
of her island talking of her husband and the farm,
the cattle they can't sell because of fears of BSE.
Like AIDS, a new disease, we say, as if the word itself could stain.
Her husband hopes for a vacation. If I were an Orcadian
what landscape would I hanker for? His choice is Malta,
small steep island just like home, but Catholic, and warm.

High Summer, Mainland

I wish for birth and it is given me. A calf thrust
from its mother at roadside onto stones and tufts
of wild grasses where low hills barely shrug away the sea

and cattle stand at home in all the green like stones.
Everything is pitched and tilted, stone or green or water:
between the harled gray houses, cylinders of silver sea

toss back the light, and you can see some other islands
but no trees. At the end of stone-paved streets
at Stromness Harbour, ships like shoals of fish,

ferries bound for Aberdeen and Bergen; local vessels
crowd the pier like cattle at salt. In thirty minutes
you can cross the island all the way to Kirkwall Harbour,

where at half-seven in high sun, I think to take the boat
to Shapinsay. A woman tells me "No, it won't return today,
it's the last sailing." When she died, her daughter left her

"That boy there," a lad about fourteen. He comes to ask
if she would like ice cream. As if he were not all she has,
she tells him no. The boat will go. She doesn't warn him

or admonish, turns to say: "We may move south. It's hard
to keep a garden going in the wind, the last
three winters have been wet and cold." In the lee

of a house rising from the hills, gable-end to the sea
I see her in the permanent wind, all that grief
and energy turned to digging sandy soil. Greens

for nourishment. And for their small delight, foxglove,
hollyhock, bright berries on long scraggly canes,
and at the verges, on their own, wild cotton,

buttercup and yarrow, daisies and pink thrift,
whatever will withstand the wind and flourish.
The boy has not returned when in the yellow light, adrift

in a long evening at the top of the world, the sky
tossing off another sunset streaked with gold,
I watch her walk onto the ferry, home.

Fleshing Stone

They say the ancient peoples who lived here
did not bury their dead, but laid them on a stone
and let the birds and animals feed. In rituals

now lost it's thought they'd gather up the bones
all mixed together, men's and women's, reedy struts
and frames of the young, and bury them in earth.

I learn this in a brace of angled slabs upright
in a field of bristly grasses spiked with wild carrot
and marsh-orchid at the solstice, the sky a thin gold

wash on silver, boiling as it does here, and the wind
grinding stone to grit. Low sun brings gifts
of history and chance: black capes snapping in the gusts,

youngsters like returning Druids leap and dance, lay flowers
at the base of standing stones at Stenness. Look north:
a pair of wild swans lifts above a blue wind-pleated loch.

Eynhallow

Peoples who lived here had built the first draft of a castle:
the great stone ring rises under black and silver skies
laden with water on a plain of brilliant springy grasses,
sea on three sides: the double-walled Broch at Gurness.

Once this was a holy place. Certain moons, or sun at solstice,
shining through a passageway across the Sound on Rousay,
came direct into the doorway here: sun lines, sacred circles,
watchstones mark moonrise. Wrapped in wind and light and mist,

Eynhallow like a fat green comma rides a hidden tidal race,
where people say like lions underneath the beds of children
currents wait to take them down. The weight of history
and wonder doesn't slow the skuas and the kittiwakes

tracking prey above the wide bright space that dazzles like a life:
long stretches of emptiness. Here and there gatherings of stones.

Tidal Island

Morsel cleft from an enormous loaf, Birsay
lies off Mainland's northwest coast in ice-slashed seas

above a few stone stacs and old whale-roads,
and you can see the weather coming on for miles.

If you cross the heaped pink slabs like broken buildings,
watch the time: high tides flood the channel, seas

engrave their fossil-stories in the stone. My guide
says once a causeway crossed what's now the little strait.

Consider causeways in the mind, this grace and time,
the ocean scintillant and wide in summer sun. Imagine God

inventing water, imagine his first seeing light
shine on it, tossing colors on the rock, green and blue

and purple, yellow. White. The world knew us.
She opened her vast burning heart. We walked inside.

Time, Grasses

On the Baltic

Whistles, foghorns, signal buoys,
funnels bellowing like whale-song

sailing over stacks of decks and shops,
my stateroom a small treasure box

with porthole onto stunning dark
and sign in Finnish: *Huom! Danger!*

Nothing frightens me, steady
in a summer storm where Vikings rode

the seas a thousand years ago. Dawn
brings rain and wind: Helsinki resolves

from dream to actuality, domes
of gold-washed silver at the far edge

of her harbor. Enormous in its coat
of startling yellow striped with white,

an icebreaker waits for winter
in thin yellow August light. A blond-gold

burly smiling man approaches me, tries
Yiddish when his English fails. Chimes

and chants and signals, gongs and carillons:
shining objects shorn of the material and ringing,

sacraments' true form. We can't know
where the years go, or what we will remember.

Rain-swept, the man on deck remains,
a figure in the mind's baroque arcade.

Bells

Easter morning. Chimes from many churches,
discordant, glorious, call across the city:
where they meet in me, little spikes of pleasure
for their echoes of far places, Russian villages

perhaps, scrubbed and picturesque. In fact
feral dogs and pigs clashed over solid matter
in the streets. Poems surround, ingest,
transform reality and leave it all

untouched. The bells loose their music, music
—I tell you—of people who have wished me dead,
and it is beautiful, iridescence laid on air, image
of a moment's memory or knowledge

—a day I walked through sounds of bells
with a man who loved me mightily and still.

Midsummer, York Minster

Ribbons of geese, the sky in violent disagreement
with itself, like churches. Downpour, sun, the rain
of concert bells over the city a glittering on air.

The open yard of the cathedral's a stage for the profane:
hubbub of tour-groups, men in medieval gear, games
erupting into laughter, lovers leaning into one another.

Voices rise through clear gold light and summer air
to the fourth floor of my hotel at the edge of a square
in the shadow of the Minster. I lean out the window

on the longest day of the last year of the millennium,
the cathedral performing one of its fundamental offices:
I am a dot at the glass in a wall of brick beneath the blue.

An archway older than my native country frames the view.
At four o'clock as if called, I fly down oddly angled stairs,
cross the square, and hesitate before the door of the cathedral.

Beneath great silent vaults of time and stone brocade
what does she feel, this woman, visitor and Jew?
As if she were a peasant, unlettered, and afraid.

St Mary's Abbey, York

*If when on a winter's night you sit feasting with your
aldermen and thanes a single sparrow should fly in one
door and swiftly out another —from winter to winter—
such it seems to me, O King, is the life of men on earth.*

—Bede

I wish you could see the grass here, bright summer green
with that odd cast clouds sometimes lay like a gauze
over the fields. The rain holds off. Birds preen
and call, cross the space between what would have been
the walls, as if they'd heard the Venerable Bede.
St Mary's Abbey's stone gleams white in the gray
afternoon light, no shadows on stone window-frames
and parts of walls, fallen columns. Nearby the Ouse
into which, eight centuries after these stones
were laid, an English gentlewoman, aging,
the war going on, and her own madness, walked,
and over whom the river, with perfect natural indifference, closed.
Wildflowers shivering in summer wind spangle
the green as they did centuries ago and then.

In Siberian Ice

What did her mother call her, little woman dead
two thousand years? And who tattooed young arms
now fixed with mythic beasts? A girl-woman
never lost is found centuries after the work
of emptying, after someone dragged tough horsehair thread
through still-fine skin to close the wounds that hadn't bled.

Water working down through mounds of stones shut her
in ice for generations. Imagine an old woman, dry
of heart, bent to do the necessary. Perhaps
she told herself, *The soul is somewhere else.* She must have
needed help to clothe her in a dress of camel's hair dyed red,
its full skirt seamed with pretty bands of other colors,

and the sash she liked, of woven rope, with tassels
she would trail across her palm, a little smile plucking
at her mouth like summer fruit. The old remember.
Who chose the blouse, dark wild silk from India,
that drifted on her skin before it stiffened;
the necklace, camels carved and layered with gold leaf?

Her tall felt headdress bears an image of the tree of life
in high country without trees. It must have been men
who laid her in the chambered grave and felled six
horses, guardians for her journey into local hills
beneath ceaseless winds. She may have been
a legendary Scythian, who, it is said, drank from skulls

of those they killed. See: they lift these, over-full of wine
in lurching light from torches, trailing strings of flesh,
to mouths smeared bright with grease at farewell feasts.

The tomb yields ancient food in painted bowls, her boots
still soft. Heaps of coriander fail to mask death's stench,
and now in open air, the wet wool smell's still fresh.

Late Summer

You start whole and end in pieces
held together by pure will
and subtle dabs of love,
as if the dispenser were almost out
of glue, as if the oil meant to burn
one night burned—a low cool flame—
just long enough to keep you warm
as necessary, your chest rising
and falling. As if the threads
holding the garment together
(that ragged shirt) were giving
up their last hold on anything,
on Europe, say, as an emigrant
to America watches the land she knows
whose language she speaks, pull away.

Above the River

Hawthornden Castle, Scotland

Light moves down the bowl of trees and fills it
with detail. Sounds of the river rise. Everywhere
this interpenetration of event: in the small room

just beyond, the serving women take their tea
and when I walk inside, domestic smells—
of laundry being done, and cooking, clean

and reassuring—the world is very close:
the Water of Esk cuts scarps into the stone
ancient trees move in and out of shadow

and now the gift of one desire: to sit and watch
all day as light moves over the glen. Birds
at altitude inhabit all of it, skies awash with weather

which like a petulant child cries and whines,
slurs soft Scots and pocks the lochs
with Gaelic in the four, the six, the endless

directions, lays hands on leafed and firred and dead
stripped trees and the ten thousand greens; beams.
As if King Midas, repenting of the stillness

but unwilling or unable to desist from his enchantment,
here and there dabbed gold on sweeps of leaves
and gilded the great trees. I want to see

what birds see as they angle down into the glen
along the river or circle north toward town
with clear untutored eye, and without longing.

Horizon

She addresses the impossible: wills herself
to come to terms with endings, books and men;
friendships wander off like errant impulse—

and where, she wants to know, does the idea
of permanence originate? Looks it up: *stay
to the end. 1526: We haue no dwellyng place ne Cite*

here permanent. Quite right: by now she's seen
histories rearrange themselves, wide streams
of rubble after avalanche, rivers cutting tracks

in stone, the lion waiting underneath the overpass.
Shadow slots the rim of the cup and troughs
of waves. Consider Venice, waiting to be taken

by the sea, the subtle mathematics
of decay as if it were a slow deliberate fanfare.

Elementary Physics

Sun-flares reach countless thousands of miles,
planets being born and dying:
why do we think we should understand anything?

We have, as children, dropped things.
They all hit the floor. Sometimes
the big people laughed. Sometimes
they were angry. We inferred from these
we could know what would happen,
that the moon would follow us home.

Intervals: Five Women

Light

Fallen leaves line the path
along the canal. Bright thread
in a tapestry, the blond girl
wearing red streaks
between the formal trees.

Place

Black sweater and pants,
bare feet on brick floor:
a blond girl plays the cello
in green light from skylights.
Covent Garden.

Time

My mother, ten and plain as bread,
climbs the hill toward home
in the dark, her violin
hitting her thigh like dread
with every step, and all her life ahead.

Then

I grieve for my daughter
after my death
little stick figure
on wide plains I'll have left.

The Power of Place

The old get smaller. Life bends them,
losses crush, fluids evaporate
and aren't replaced, and this is true
but not enough. It is the power of place with them
they drag on their backs, kitchens
lit with yellow light, dark passageways
to beds drenched with sex or fever
or the terrible hanging on: every place
they've been and all they haven't,
concert halls and concentration camps,
each with its own sound, each
its own peculiar light. If you lay your cheek
or press the palm of your hand
against the walls in old houses
you can hear the murmuring. You want
to forget they were joined in slavery
or built on trade, you want to rock the babies
buried without names, generations
of boy-soldiers. You lean
against the lamentations in the walls,
you brush your lips against the boards, you want
to touch them so long dead, you want
to whisper, *Rest, rest. Enough.*

Time, Grasses: Reprise

It is glorious and difficult. You cannot possibly
take it all in, though your eyes reach
—if they were mouths, ravenous, if hands,
extended, all the tendons taut—*zing*
of longing in your fingertips and on your lips.
If you could hold on, remember all of it—?
You know. You only get to do it once.

It's near the end of all the days.
If you walk east you walk into the dark.
Turn your back on the sun. Hard as it is, turn
away. As if there were a hand pressing
on your back, it is not possible to stay.
And anyway it heaves and breathes,
the lessening, and finally gathers everything.

Prudencia in the Blue Synagogue

We are astonishingly thin
in goodness, fine china cups
glowing in the light through them.

Sometimes she remembers the porcelain
is made of ground and heated bone.
We are all there is. She gazes

at the altar. If she had been adopted
what would her true faith be? At home
all the fragrant places of her youth

have been paved over. Woman, split
pink softness, man thick and thickening
baton. She considers rapture.

It takes the breath how little shows,
as when, the door blown open
in a gust, her loved one had become

a great black shadow in a shattering of light.
All our lives we make a kind of raw theology,
learning as we go, a few fine acts in long lives

filled with lies, self-interest, futile
sacrifice. We are frail in loving
despite tales of mothers lifting cars

from children, returning to the burning house.
We are easily crushed, torn, broken,
burned, dismembered. Like pumpkins thrown

from backs of trucks, we split and shatter.
All of it has happened. None of it
has failed to happen. It isn't possible

to learn how not to torment one another.
Even if we knew the wrongs, we wouldn't fail
next time. Hurt stacks up like skulls

in medieval towers. The losses are of everything
and are insupportable, and life
the pitiless dream we can't wake from.

Notes

"Three Small Songs": "I mean the years are like a lead fence." —HD: *HERmione*, New Directions, 1981; 97.

"Disquisition on Yellow": The cartoon and quote are in Cecelia Powell, *Turner,* The Pitkin Guide, Norwich, England: Jarrold Publishing, 2003.

1819, Blackwoods: "A new and beautiful yellow pigment" appears in the OED online.

1923 book is *The Enjoyment and Use of Color,* Walter Sargent. New York: Dover Publications.

Painted Labyrinth: The World of the Lindisfarne Gospels, Michelle P. Brown, London: The British Library, 2003.

Clay and Glazes for the Potter, Revised Edition, Daniel Rhodes, Radnor, PA: Chilton Book Company, 1973.

Borges, *This Craft of Verse,* The Charles Eliot Norton Lectures, 1967–1968. Cambridge, MA: Harvard University Press, 2000; afterword by Editor Calin-Andrei Mihailescu, 147.

"The Sun in Ultraviolet Light": The Rose Center, The Museum of Natural History, New York, March 2000.

Other notes are from *Nova* (PBS), and newspaper articles ("Science Times," *The New York Times*), various dates. All quotations have been modified to suit the poem.

"The Archimedes Palimpsest" : The pages were found in 1906 and again in 1971 (*Nova*, December 2003).

"Photograph: *Am Naschmarkt*": The photo appears in *Vienna 1890–1920*, ed. Robert Waissenberger, Keep Library, Hawthornden Castle, Scotland.

"Orkney Crossing":

"KOI": Kirkwall, Orkney Islands; "inches of land": *inch* is Scots'

Gaelic for "island" and refers here to the islands dotting Loch Ness, which cuts the country on a diagonal northeast to southwest.

"A Few Facts": BSE is bovine spongiform encephalopathy, mad cow disease, the virulent illness that required British farmers to kill thousands of cattle in the mid- to late-1990s. Hazel and her husband's cattle turned out to be free of infection.

"Mainland": People who live on Orkney call their largest island Mainland. Most of the names of islands in the Orkney group end in "ay," pronounced "ee," which means "island"; Shapinsay is pronounced Shapinzee. *Kirkwall* comes from the Old Norse *Kirkjuvagr:* Kirk (or Church) Bay (vag, voe, hope).

"Eynhallow" : *-ness* in place-names, here Gurness, means "headland." The accent in this particular case falls on the first syllable: *Gur*-ness. The Broch is "a late prehistoric structure (dating *chf* from the first century BC and the first two centuries AD), found *chf* in Ork and Sh, the *Western Isles* . . . and the adjacent Scottish mainland, consisting of a large round tower with hollow stone-built walls . . ." (*The Concise Scots Dictionary*). The Broch of Gurness is thought to be two thousand years old. The strait between Eynhallow and the other islands is called the "roosh," "rush" in Scots, and may also refer to "Burgher Roost," which is what the people living there call the Eynhallow coast facing the strait; *eyn* is derived from Old English, "egg," information for which I'm indebted to my friend George Petty.

"In Siberian Ice" : "The soul is somewhere else" is attributed by the *Nando Times* (1997) to the husband of the archaeologist, Natalya Polosmak, who found the grave in 1993.

"Horizon": The quoted material is from the OED.

"Prudencia in the Blue Synagogue" : The phrase *blue synagogue* appears in a poem by Donald Hall.

Acknowledgments

With appreciation to the editors who first published these poems, often in a different version:

Big Muddy: Journal of the Mississippi River Valley: "Holy Saturday in the Northern Plains";

The Comstock Review: "Fictions of Place–Time";

Harvard Magazine: "The Power of Place" (reprinted in *Claiming the Spirit Within*);

Icarus International: "Child on an Airplane";

Kestrel: "In Siberian Ice," "I Sleep with a Man I Don't Love," "Optics";

Near East Review (Ankara; Riyadh): "Bright Yellow Square: Laib's Pollen," "Out of the Garden" (as "Fields, North America");

Never Before: Poems about First Experiences: "Cathedral" (first published in *Two Rivers Review*);

NYCBigCityLit.com: "Above Half-Moon Bay," "Arnold's Meadow";

Poems and Plays: "The Dead Child";

Poetry International: "Inlet, Duluth";

Rattapallax: "Guide to the Cathedral," "Midsummer, York Minster";

Smartish Pace: "Late Summer," "Two Poppies";

The Southern Review: "St Mary's Abbey, York";

Summer Shade: "3 Men: Portraits Without the Human Figure";

Two Rivers Review: "Cathedral," "Generation," "Intervals: Five Women."

"Trees in Ice" appeared at the Peconic Gallery, a visual arts & poetry exhibit on the theme of hope, curated by Marvin Bell.

"Above the River" received special recognition from the New England Poetry Club.

The author wishes to express her deep appreciation to The Baltic Centre for Writers and Translators, Hawthornden Castle, and Yaddo.

She also wishes to thank Montclair State University for time given through its Faculty Scholarship Incentive Program.

Warmest thanks to George, Carol, Charlotte, Carol, Kay, Phil, Tom, Chris, Chet, Sharon, Laure-Anne, Gayle and Joffy. Hearfelt appreciation to Alicia and Michael and George; to Thom; and to Anique Taylor for her cover artwork. And as ever great thanks to Aimée, Molly, Don.

About the Author

Deena Linett has published prize-winning novels and short fiction. This is her second collection of poems.

In Summer 2004 she was resident at The Centre for Writers and Translators on Gotland, in the Baltic Sea, and has twice had fellowships to Hawthornden Castle, Scotland, and to Yaddo.

Linett, the mother of three children, is Professor of English at Montclair State University. She serves as Associate Editor at *Near East Review* (Riyadh) and frequently collaborates with Chicago weaver Aimée Picard.

BOA Editions, Ltd., American Poets Continuum Series

Colophon

Woman Crossing a Field, poems by Deena Linett,
is set in Bernhard Modern and ITC Officina Sans Book
with text design by Richard Foerster, York Beach, Maine.
The cover design is by Lisa Mauro. The cover art,
"VanBuskirk Angel" by Anique Taylor, is courtesy of the artist.
Manufacturing is by McNaughton & Gunn, Lithographers,
Saline Michigan.

The publication of this book is made possible, in part,
by the special support of the following individuals:

Angela Bonazinga & Catherine Lewis
Alan & Nancy Cameros
City Blue Imaging
Gwen & Gary Conners
Burch & Louise Craig
Peter & Suzanne Durant
Bev & Pete French
Dane & Judy Gordon
Kip & Deb Hale
Noel Hanlon & Peter Koehler, Jr.
Tom & Illona Hansen
Peter & Robin Hursh
Robert & Willy Hursh
X. J. Kennedy
Archie & Pat Kutz
Rosemary & Lew Lloyd
Philip Memmer & Michelle Reiser-Memmer
Jimmy & Wendy Mnookin
Boo Poulin
James Robie & Edith Matthai
David & Ellen Wallack
Pat & Michael Wilder